Fact Finders®

The Story of
Sanitation

RUNNING
WATER!

HOW DOES
WATER GET
INTO OUR TAPS?

by Riley Flynn

raintree
a Capstone company — publishers for children

Raintree is an imprint of Capstone Global Library Limited, a company incorporated in England and Wales having its registered office at 264 Banbury Road, Oxford, OX2 7DY – Registered company number: 6695582

www.raintree.co.uk
myorders@raintree.co.uk

Edited by Anna Butzer
Designed by Bobbie Nuytten
Original illustrations © Capstone Global Library Limited 2019
Picture research by Morgan Walters
Production by Kris Wilfahrt
Originated by Capstone Global Library Ltd
Printed and bound in India

ISBN 978 1 4747 6424 7
22 21 20 19 18
10 9 8 7 6 5 4 3 2 1

British Library Cataloguing in Publication Data
A full catalogue record for this book is available from the British Library.

Acknowledgements
We would like to thank the following for permission to reproduce photographs: Capstone Press: Alison Theile, 18-19; Newscom: DISABILITYIMAGES\SCIENCE PHOTO LIBRARY, 12, Historica Graphica Collection Heritage Images, 11; Shutterstock: aleksander hunta, 20, brian legate, 22, Deyan Georgiev, 4, DiKiYaqua, 9, hedgehog94, 6, HUKEEHOM, (droplet) Cover, design element throughout, I WALL, (paper) design element throughout, JJJSINA, 25, johavel, 7, John1179, 24, Lisa S, 23, NatashaPhoto, 13, nito, 10, 28, OMMB, 16, Pablo Prat, 21, photopixel, (faucet) Cover, Robert Kneschke, 5, 29, SetSailPhoto, 27, Sukan Saythong, (filters) Cover, W.Tab, 14-15, 17, Yuri Samsonov, 1

CONTENTS

CHAPTER 1
ALL ABOUT WATER

We use water for so many different things every day. We clean our houses and our bodies with it. We drink it and use it to flush our toilets. We water our crops and cook with it. Without enough clean water, our towns and cities would be dirty and smelly. The world would be filled with dead plants and very thirsty people.

Farmers use large sprinkler systems to water crops.

We need water to live because our bodies are 60 per cent water. Finding water and making it clean is important for everyone. **Purified** drinking water hasn't been around very long. For thousands of years, humans drank water that stank, tasted horrible and made them sick. In fact, in some countries, people still can't get clean drinking water.

HYDRATION IS HEALTHY

Water is the key to staying hydrated (keeping a healthy amount of fluids in our bodies). When we sweat, our bodies lose water, so it's important to drink water when you're being active. But we also lose water from our bodies whenever we breathe or go to the toilet. It's important to replace those fluids by drinking water every day. To stay healthy, you need to drink about 1.2 litres (6 to 8 glasses) of water a day.

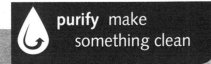

purify make something clean

5

People have worked hard to keep your drinking water safe. Thousands of engineers are working this very minute. They pipe water into treatment centres, purify it and pipe it to your house. Now if you turn on the tap, clean water comes out.

The United States uses more than 1.5 trillion litres (402 billion gallons) of water per day. That's more than any other country in the world. Countries such as the United States are making efforts to reduce the amount of water they consume. As populations around the world continue to grow, we must conserve this vital resource to ensure there is enough water for everyone.

About 200 billion plastic water bottles are used around the world each year.

WATER, WATER, EVERYWHERE?

Water is being used faster than it can be replaced in some parts of the world. In the UK, the average person uses 150 litres (40 gallons) of water per day. Here's how that water is usually used:

30%
flushing the toilet

7%
outside
(garden taps and hoses)

21%
washing clothes

5%
other

8%
washing up

25%
washing people
(showers or baths)

4%
drinking water

CHAPTER 2
THIRSTY PEOPLE IN HISTORY

In ancient times people didn't know about germs. But they did know that dirty water could make them unwell. As the number of people on the planet grew, it became harder to get clean water to everyone. So what did people do? They thought of new ways to clean water and take it to people.

Intelligent Indians

In ancient India, people didn't know what germs were. But they still found a way to stop getting ill from dirty water. Ancient Indians heated water until it boiled. Then they filtered it by pouring it through sand and gravel. Both of these techniques clean water. Boiling water kills germs, and filtering clears out other unpleasant stuff.

Boiling water kills germs and parasites. It is the safest method of purifying water.

CLEAN COINCIDENCE

Around 400 BC a Greek physician called Hippocrates discovered ways to improve drinking water. At this time, the quality of water was determined by its smell, taste and appearance. Hippocrates found that boiling water removed the nasty smells and tastes. He didn't realize that it also removed germs that could cause diseases.

Roman plumbing

The Romans built **aqueducts** to carry water into their cities. These stone waterways transported water from one place to another. Romans didn't have electricity to power their aqueducts, so they used **gravity**.

The aqueducts started at the top of mountains. Streams flowing down the mountains poured into the aqueducts.

aqueduct large bridge built to carry water from a mountain into a valley

gravity force that pulls objects with mass together

At one point, Rome had 11 aqueducts. The longest aqueduct was 95 kilometres (59 miles).

The aqueducts delivered water to wells and pipes. The water passed through clay and sand filters to clean it. Some of the water was piped into the homes of the emperor and other rich people. The rest went to public fountains, where common people could fill their buckets.

As time went on, the ideas of the ancient Indians and Romans disappeared. When wars broke out, large sections of the Roman aqueducts were ruined during attacks on Rome. After that, Romans got their water from local rivers.

Once the Roman aqueducts were no longer usable, people used polluted river water.

CHAPTER 3

FROM STREAM TO STORAGE

We've learned a lot about cleaning water since ancient times. Scientists from many different fields have taught us about **bacteria** and harmful chemicals. They've also discovered how to get rid of germs.

Today, water is tested, treated and cleaned so it's safe to drink. **Lab technicians** at water treatment centres have learned the best ways to clean water. Water goes through a series of steps to be cleaned.

FACT The most common steps in water treatment are coagulation, sedimentation, filtration, disinfection and storage.

Lab technicians at water treatment plants make sure our drinking water is free of bacteria and waste.

Water is pumped from a water source and moved through pipes to a water treatment centre. Then the first step in water treatment, **coagulation**, begins. Chemicals that act like magnets are added to the water. These chemicals make all the dirt particles in the water clump together (coagulate).

This process was invented by the ancient Egyptians. Amazingly, after thousands of years, technicians use the same chemical the ancient Egyptians used – **alum**. Technicians today add some other chemicals, too, but alum is still the main ingredient.

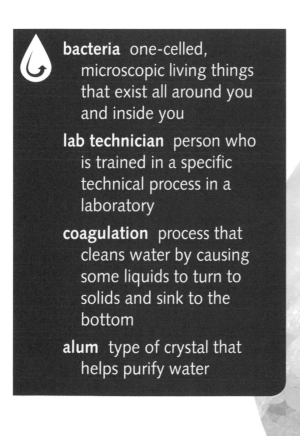

bacteria one-celled, microscopic living things that exist all around you and inside you

lab technician person who is trained in a specific technical process in a laboratory

coagulation process that cleans water by causing some liquids to turn to solids and sink to the bottom

alum type of crystal that helps purify water

Alum (aluminium sulphate) is widely used for water treatment.

As the dirt clumps stick together, they become heavy and sink to the bottom of the water. This part of water treatment is called **sedimentation**. Then the clear water on top is pushed through a series of filters. These filters are made out of sand, gravel or charcoal. They remove the smallest specks of dust, bacteria and chemicals.

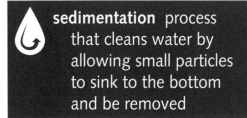

sedimentation process that cleans water by allowing small particles to sink to the bottom and be removed

Sedimentation tanks get a bit of help from gravity. The particles get heavy and sink to the bottom of the tank.

Disinfection

The next step is disinfection. This process can be done in two different ways. Usually an **element** called **chlorine** is added to the water to kill any remaining germs. This chemical element is also used in swimming pools to stop bacteria turning the water green.

Scientists know that chlorine breaks down into other chemicals that are harmful to fish. They think these same chemicals may not be good for humans either. Some treatment facilities are now using **ultraviolet light** instead of chlorine in their water treatment process.

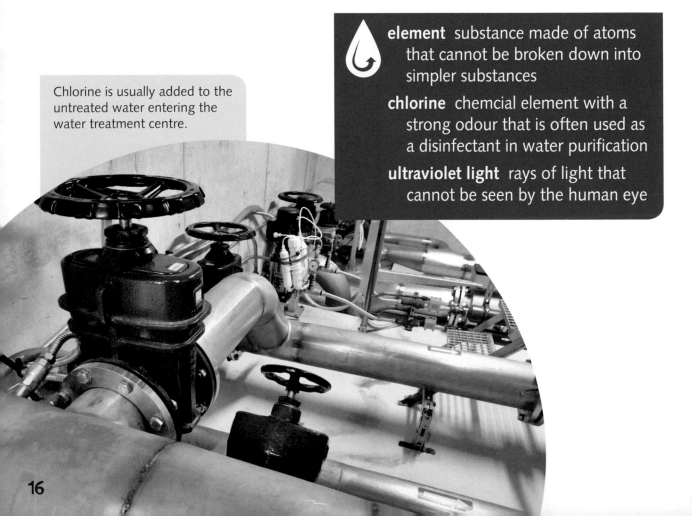

Chlorine is usually added to the untreated water entering the water treatment centre.

element substance made of atoms that cannot be broken down into simpler substances

chlorine chemcial element with a strong odour that is often used as a disinfectant in water purification

ultraviolet light rays of light that cannot be seen by the human eye

Ultraviolet light waves can be harmful and cause sunburn. But those same light waves can also kill germs that make us ill. Lastly, water goes into storage until people need to use it. In some countries water is stored in huge water towers. In other countries, it is stored in underground holding tanks.

Water treatment centres use a minimum of three different filters to clean water.

The treatment train

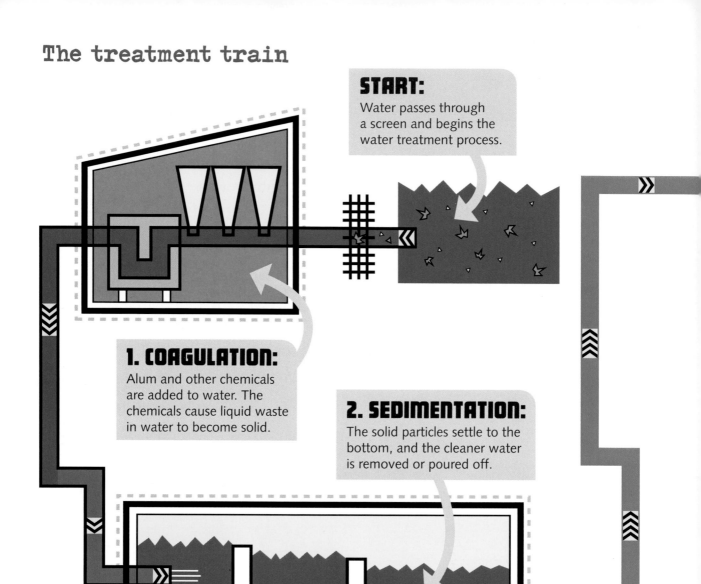

START:
Water passes through a screen and begins the water treatment process.

1. COAGULATION:
Alum and other chemicals are added to water. The chemicals cause liquid waste in water to become solid.

2. SEDIMENTATION:
The solid particles settle to the bottom, and the cleaner water is removed or poured off.

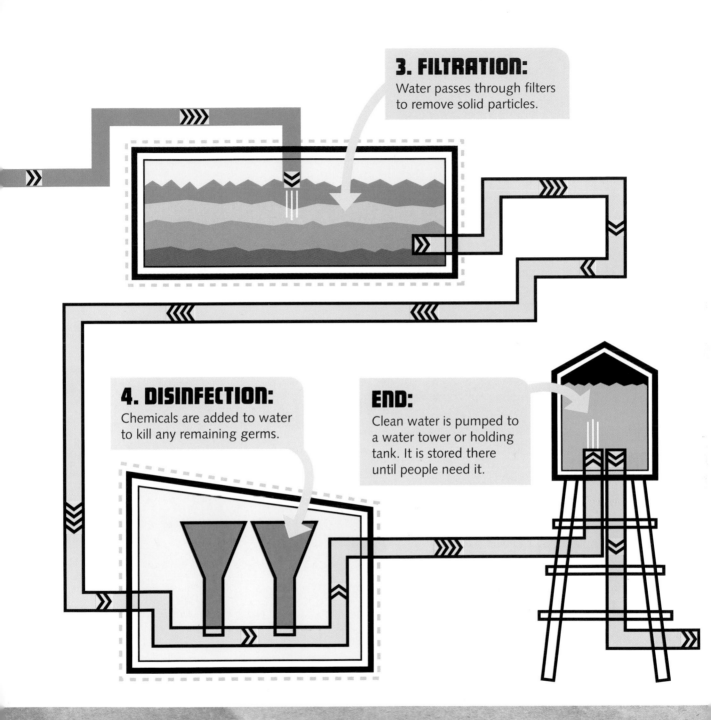

3. FILTRATION:
Water passes through filters to remove solid particles.

4. DISINFECTION:
Chemicals are added to water to kill any remaining germs.

END:
Clean water is pumped to a water tower or holding tank. It is stored there until people need it.

Where does water come from?

Humans use two types of water – groundwater and surface water. Surface water comes from streams, rivers, lakes and **reservoirs**. Groundwater is found underground.

Even water that looks clear and clean can have germs in it.

Groundwater is formed when water seeps into the ground and collects in **aquifers**. People dig wells to reach aquifers. Shallow wells are around 15 metres (50 feet) deep. Bigger wells can go down 300 metres (984 feet) or more. The deeper the well, the cleaner the water.

When water travels down that far, it passes through lots of sand, rock and soil. These materials naturally filter the water. Unfortunately, you can't replace groundwater. Once an aquifer or a well is empty, there is no way to refill it.

Depending on where the water is coming from, it is treated (cleaned) in different ways. But both surface water and groundwater can become **contaminated**.

Reservoirs are man-made bodies of water. They are usually created in areas where there are not many lakes to supply safe drinking water.

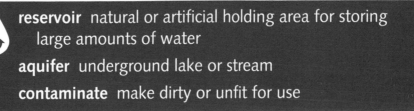

reservoir natural or artificial holding area for storing large amounts of water

aquifer underground lake or stream

contaminate make dirty or unfit for use

No matter where our water comes from, it is affected by what happens on the land around it. Sometimes, when it rains a lot, water can no longer soak into the ground. When this happens, the rainwater travels to a water source as **run-off**. The run-off picks up **pollutants** on its way to rivers, streams and lakes. Some of these pollutants contaminate our water sources.

We all contribute to the contamination of our water. Most of the time we don't even realize that we're doing it. We contribute to water contamination if we use toxic cleaning products or forget to pick up our dog's poo!

A water drainage pipe empties out into nature.

run-off rain that is not absorbed by the soil

pollutant harmful material that can damage the environment

Contamination of our water sources can cause diseases. Sometimes a contaminated water source can become impossible to clean, and the source can no longer be used. Polluted run-off is the number one cause of water quality problems today.

The amount of run-off water is even higher when there is heavy rain.

CHAPTER 4

PROTECTING OUR WATER

Did you know there are laws in place to help protect water? These laws protect water sources and help keep water clean. There are also laws that limit the amount of water we can use on our lawns and gardens. Because water is easy to access, some people don't think about how much they are using.

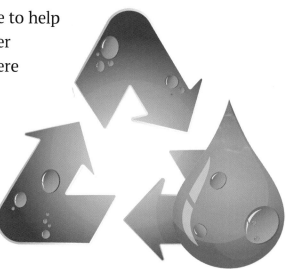

WATER WITH RULES

In the UK, the quality of our drinking water is carefully monitored in line with guidelines from WHO (World Health Organization). These guidelines are regularly updated to keep up with scientific discoveries and advances in technology. Regulations similar to these are put in place across the world so everyone can have safe drinking water.

Water is a limited resource, so **conserving** it is very important. There are many simple ways to save water. We can turn the water off while brushing our teeth, have quicker showers and make sure none of our taps are leaking.

FACT Ask your parents to help you test for leaks by placing a drop of food colouring in your toilet cistern. If the colour appears in the toilet bowl without flushing, you have a leak!

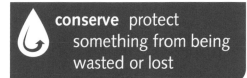

conserve protect something from being wasted or lost

Next time you turn on a tap, remember that 844 million people in the world don't have clean water close to home.

City planners and engineers work hard to find the cleanest water sources possible. They make sure that factories aren't dumping waste into reservoirs. They clean the water from sewer systems before pumping it back into rivers. They test for chemicals and poisons before the water even gets to the treatment plant. No matter how clean a water source looks, water is not safe to drink until it has been treated.

We all need water to survive. That's why engineers are filtering, cleaning and pumping water right now. Many cities have thousands of litres of water in underground holding tanks or water towers. It's just waiting for someone to turn on the tap and have a drink.

Water towers are often made of concrete, steel or brick.

FACT Water towers are used to hold water for the town or community they are near. Water towers hold about a day's worth of water. For most water towers, that is about 3.8 million litres (1 million gallons).

TIMELINE

312 BC
The first Roman aqueduct is built.

1746
The first widely used water filter was created. It was made of wool, sponges and charcoal.

1804
Paisley in Scotland becomes the first city in the world to provide filtered water for the entire city.

1829
James Simpson of the Chelsea Waterworks Company introduces the slow sand filtration system to supply treated water to the people of London.

1908
Water treatment plants in the USA start using chlorine to treat water.

300 BC   **1500**   **1900**

1980

The United Nations declares the start of the International Drinking Water Decade. They hope to bring attention and support for clean water worldwide.

1970

The Environmental Protection Agency (EPA) is established in the United States.

1974

US Congress passes the Safe Drinking Water Act to help protect the USA's drinking water.

1990

The Drinking Water Inspectorate (DWI) is formed to ensure that water supplies in England and Wales are clean and safe to drink.

1970

1990

GLOSSARY

alum type of crystal that helps purify water

aqueduct large bridge built to carry water from a mountain into a valley

aquifer underground lake or stream

bacteria one-celled, microscopic living things that exist all around you and inside you; many bacteria are useful, but some cause disease

chlorine chemical element with a strong odour that is often used as a disinfectant in water purification

coagulation process that cleans water by causing some liquids to turn to solids and sink to the bottom

conserve protect something from being wasted or lost

contaminate make dirty or unfit for use

element substance made of atoms that cannot be broken down into simpler substances

gravity force that pulls objects with mass together; gravity pulls objects down towards the centre of Earth

lab technician person who is trained in a specific technical process in a laboratory

pollutant harmful material that can damage the environment

purify make something clean

reservoir natural or artificial holding area for storing large amounts of water

run-off rain that is not absorbed by the soil

sedimentation process that cleans water by allowing small particles to sink to the bottom and be removed

ultraviolet light rays of light that cannot be seen by the human eye

FIND OUT MORE

BOOKS

Environment Infographics (Infographics), Chris Oxlade (Raintree, 2015)

The Science Behind the Wonders of the Water (The Science Behind Natural Phenomena), Suzanne Garbe (Raintree, 2017)

Science vs Disease (Science Fights Back), Matthew Anniss (Raintree, 2017)

The Water Cycle (Earth by Numbers), Nancy Dickmann (Raintree, 2018)

WEBSITES

Find out how the water cycle works at:
www.dkfindout.com/uk/earth/water-cycle/how-does-water-cycle-work

Discover some useful tips on how to save water and learn more about your water supply at:
news.bbc.co.uk/cbbcnews/hi/newsid_4800000/newsid_4806400/4806478.stm

COMPREHENSION QUESTIONS

1. What are some ways we can help keep our water sources clean?

2. Why is it important that every person on Earth has access to clean water?

3. Look at the information on page 7. What are some ways you can reduce the amount of water you use?

INDEX